I0159507

IF I WERE YOUNG AGAIN:
Hints From My Sixty Years For Those That Have Sixty Years Ahead of Them

By
AMOS R. WELLS

First Fruits Press
Wilmore, Kentucky
c2016

If I were young again : hints from my sixty years for those that have sixty years
ahead of them.
By Amos R. Wells.

First Fruits Press, ©2016

Previously published by Westminster Press, 1929.

ISBN: 9781621715412 (print) 9781621715429 (digital) 9781621715436 (kindle)

Digital version at http://place.asburyseminary.edu/christianendeavorbooks/44/

First Fruits Press is a digital imprint of the Asbury Theological Seminary, B.L.
Fisher Library. Asbury Theological Seminary is the legal owner of the material
previously published by the Pentecostal Publishing Co. and reserves the right to
release new editions of this material as well as new material produced by Asbury
Theological Seminary. Its publications are available for noncommercial and
educational uses, such as research, teaching and private study. First Fruits Press
has licensed the digital version of this work under the Creative Commons
Attribution Noncommercial 3.0 United States License. To view a copy of this
license, visit http://creativecommons.org/licenses/by-nc/3.0/us/.

For all other uses, contact:

First Fruits Press
B.L. Fisher Library
Asbury Theological Seminary
204 N. Lexington Ave.
Wilmore, KY 40390
http://place.asburyseminary.edu/firstfruits

Wells, Amos R. (Amos Russel), 1862-1933.

If I were young again : hints from my sixty years for those that have sixty
years ahead of them / by Amos R. Wells. Wilmore, Kentucky : First Fruits
Press, ©2016.
40 pages ; 21 cm.

Reprint. Previously published: Philadelphia : Westminster Press, 1929.

I would build up a strong body -- I would commit more to memory -- I would
practice public speaking -- I would learn one thing well -- I would train my
hands -- I would become expert in some sport -- I would read more
methodically -- I would select my calling earlier -- I would join the church
earlier -- I would live for larger interests -- I would work more for others -- I
would give time to soul nurture.

ISBN - 13: 9781621715412 (paperback)

1. Youth--Conduct of Life. 2. Conduct of life. 3. Self-culture. 4. Success. I.
Title.

BJ1595 .W45 2016

Cover design by Jonathan Ramsay

asburyseminary.edu
800.2ASBURY
204 North Lexington Avenue
Wilmore, Kentucky 40390

First Fruits
THE ACADEMIC OPEN PRESS OF ASBURY SEMINARY

First Fruits Press
The Academic Open Press of Asbury Theological Seminary
204 N. Lexington Ave., Wilmore, KY 40390
859-858-2236
first.fruits@asburyseminary.edu
asbury.to/firstfruits

IF I WERE YOUNG AGAIN

HINTS FROM MY SIXTY YEARS FOR THOSE THAT HAVE SIXTY YEARS AHEAD OF THEM

BY

AMOS R. WELLS, LITT. D., LL.D.

PHILADELPHIA
THE WESTMINSTER PRESS
1929

Copyright, 1924
By F. M. Braselman

Printed in the United States of America

PREFACE

WHEN I was a young fellow, starting out on the journey which now has covered sixty years, I was greatly interested in such books as Edward Everett Hale's "How to Do It," Samuel Smiles's "Self-Help," and William Mathews's "Getting On in the World." Books of that sort, giving young folks glimpses of the road that lies before them, and telling them how they can travel over the road most quickly and easily to reach their goal, are eagerly read by boys and girls, young men and young women, who are by no means the careless and reckless creatures they sometimes think it necessary to appear to be.

This is a book of the same kind, but its viewpoint is a little different. Instead of inviting my readers to look ahead over their own routes, I am asking them to stand at my side and look back over my path, while I point out some mistakes I have made in choosing my course. For the roads through life, though seeming to be so various and different, are after all very much alike, and the same temptations to turn from the best way that came to me will be sure to come to each one of you. I have seen enough of life to be certain that you will be the gainers from the survey that I propose, and that it will enable you to avoid many a bypath that leads to no good end or to an end only second best. So come, young comrades, eager to get ahead, and spend an hour or two looking backward with me. Then forward on your own ways, and God bless you all!

Boston, Massachusetts   AMOS R. WELLS

CONTENTS

If I Were Young Again—

I

If I Were Young Again

I Would Build Up a Strong Body

HAVING reached the goodly age of sixty, I am inclined to look backward and review my past life. In doing so, I often think of matters which I would manage differently if I could do them over again, and some of those matters I will speak about in this series of chapters. Perhaps the reading of them will lead the readers of this book to avoid my mistakes, to their vast betterment.

And in the first place, if I were young once more, I would build up a strong body. Like most other boys in Ohio six decades ago, I never thought about my health, either present or future. I ate what I felt like eating, and when the headaches came, as they often did, I had a horrible time, and wondered why headaches were allowed in the world. The result was that indigestion got its grip upon me, and almost ruined years of my life before I got the better of it.

I did not take decent care of my teeth, and those indispensable tools of health, strength, and happiness fell into sad decay, keeping me poor with dentists' bills, holding me for many years spasmodically on the rack of toothache, and leaving me with a very inferior dental apparatus for preparing the fuel of life's engine.

As to exercise, I was just as big a fool. I took a walk—when I wanted to find fossils. I took runs—to catch butterflies. I got on a trapeze once, but I fell off and cut a hole in my hand. I got on a horse once, but I fell off and broke my wrist. I rode a bicycle, but I fell off and broke the other wrist. I played tennis, but not enough to play half well. I played baseball once, and got hit in my nearsighted eyes, my glasses being broken.

I played football once, with the same result precisely. Then I took to croquet.

The result of it all was that I came to manhood with a body absurdly inadequate to the very heavy demands I made upon it, and have had to struggle with physical weakness for many years.

I have learned, by miserable experience, a few rules and methods for the management of the body which would have been of priceless value to me when I was young—if I had had the sense to heed them. Little rules like these: Never eat too much. Go easy on candy and soda water. Chew your food thoroughly. Eat a variety of substantials. Choose some outdoor exercise or sport and become proficient in it. Live outdoors two hours every day. Go to bed with the sun when you can, and get up with the same—or earlier. Stand up straight (I never knew how to do it until I married a gymnasium director). Sit up straight. Take pains to get rid of the waste materials of the body. Brush your teeth assiduously after every meal. Never read in a poor light, or a minute after your eyes begin to hurt.

Of course these things were all told me when I was young, but I did not really hear them until I began to grow old. I did just what I hope you who are reading this will *not* do; I said, "Just this once won't do any harm." And "just this once," multiplied by three hundred and sixty-five days a year, *did* do harm, lots of it.

Almost everybody, on reaching the age of sixty, realizes painfully the entire truth of all that I have been saying. The big problem is to get the young folks to realize it while the knowledge will do the most good, while it is not too late to build up a strong body. That need not be a problem in your case.

A strong body is not to be had by chance. It must be planned for. It will not do to go into athletics just to beat some other school, taking up some sport that may do your body more harm than good. You are given a mind in order that you may use reason and direct your life along wise channels. Determine for yourself what your body needs to transform its weakness into strength, and then do that thing as persistently as young Theodore Roosevelt trained his feeble body at Harvard and came out one of the strongest men of his day.

And so I really think that if I could live my life over again I should plan for a strong body, and see that the plan was carried out. Bodily health is not the greatest thing in the world, but there is no great thing which is not more easily attained by its aid, and used to better purpose when we have it to help. You at sixteen, heed the word of sixty!

II

If I Were Young Again

I Would Commit More to Memory

WHEN I was young, no one told me that I was then at the age of easy memorizing. No one spurred me on to fill my mind with choice pieces of prose and poetry on the ground that they would be a wonderful resource all through my life, and that I should never again be able to commit to memory so easily.

The result was that I stored away in my mind only the few parts of the Bible that I was made to learn in the Sunday school, and only the few poems (and no prose) that I was made to recite in the public school. Since then, to be sure, I have added to my memory treasures in a desultory fashion, but very little that can be depended upon.

If I had my youth again, let me tell you what I would do with my memory.

In the first place, I would commit to memory at least one Bible verse every day. Sometimes they would be isolated verses, sometimes they would make up a great Bible passage. I would often review them and make sure of them.

In that way I would get a lifelong grip on perhaps fifty of the psalms, on the Sermon on the Mount, on Christ's last discourse and prayer, on the leading parables, and on the great chapters of the Epistles such as Romans 12, First Corinthians 13 and 15, and Hebrews 11. I would select a string of Bible verses all on the same topic, such as prayer, or heaven, or patience, or forgiveness, or temptation, and fasten them in my mind ready for instant use in my own life or in the lives of others. A verse a day for the ten years between the years of eight and eighteen, say, would have given me a priceless capital of thirty-six hundred and fifty Bible verses, the equivalent of perhaps one hundred chapters. I do not dare to think what that would have meant for me and for my work in the world—the comfort, the guidance, and the power. And it would have been so easy and so pleasant!

Then, turning to secular literature, I would commit a lot of it to memory if I could live my boyhood over again.

I would begin with poetry, because that is the easier, but I would not at all neglect the great prose. I would commit to memory, of course, the poems I liked, but I would try to like the best poems, those chosen by good judges to make up the choicest collections of poems.

These poems would seldom be narrative poems. Those were almost the only poems I was made to recite in school, because they afforded the best chance to display "elocution"; but the rhymed stories that I declaimed so vigorously have been of no use to me in after years, whereas if I had committed to memory great compositions like Wordsworth's "Ode on the Intimations of Immortality," Lowell's "Commemoration Ode," Gray's "Elegy," and the best portions of Tennyson's "In Memoriam," I should have found those memory treasures of constant value. Shakespeare should have been read by me with an eye to the many memorable passages; and these alone, if thus stored away, would have been an incomparable inspiration. Much of Milton is equally fruitful; yes, and the whole of such poems as Goldsmith's "The Traveller" and "The Deserted Village," nearly every line of which has furnished a common quotation.

But there are hundreds of poems, long and short, that do not deserve memorizing in their entirety, merely a central stanza or sometimes only a single superlative line. I should have been on the watch for these.

And hymns! Almost above all that I have named of great poetry I would name the great hymns. How I wish that I had made them my own in boyhood, so that

IF I WERE YOUNG AGAIN

I could now sing them over in the dark, by myself, at midnight periods of wakefulness, in times of lonely grief, or whenever a hymn book is not at hand. As it is, I can usually get through the first stanza without printed help, and then comes chaos.

And finally, I wish I had stored in my mind some of the great prose—hundreds of wise and inspiring isolated sentences, and great passages from the world's masterly state papers and epochal orations and sermons. The field here is endless, and I should have been tempted at every turn to do more than time would allow; but a single sentence culled from a masterpiece, if only one each week, would by this time have enriched my mind and soul beyond measure.

Those that read these words may easily, if they will, make themselves millionaires of thought. Great wealth is ready for you, in the world's great books. Will you not take it, and make it your own for life?

III

If I Were Young Again

I Would Practice Public Speaking

ONE of my regrets as, from my sixtieth birthday, I look back upon my younger days, is that I did not avail myself then of my many opportunities to practice public speaking. Whenever, in the public school or college, I had a choice between debating or writing and reading an essay, I always chose the essay. When I was forced to debate, I wrote out and read as much of my argument as possible. Whenever I knew in advance that I should be called upon to speak in my literary society, I wrote out something and laboriously committed it to memory. After graduation I went into the college faculty and was called upon to take my turn in conducting the chapel exercises; but my remarks were always written and read. I joined the Christian Endeavor Society and was loyal to my pledge, but my contribution to each meeting was the inevitable bit of written paper. If I had to lead a meeting, my "opening remarks" were composed in advance and painstakingly read. When I began teaching in the Sunday school, I wrote out every question I was to ask, and fired it at the class from manuscript. When I came into the national Christian Endeavor work and had often to address conventions, a manuscript came between me and my audience, or I would commit my speech to memory with horrible toil and deliver it with inward quakings for fear I should forget the next sentence. It was all a slavish dependence upon pencil and paper. My public work lacked manhood, independence, and effectiveness. No one can be forceful whose mind may go blank at any instant. No one can impress himself upon an audience when he is manifestly giving them not what he is now thinking, but what he thought and wrote down yesterday or last week.

If I Were Young Again

I have come to see the error of my ways, and have brought myself with much labor and many fears to the power of more or less extemporaneous speaking. I can address an audience without flinching, if I have to, and if I have had no previous notice and no chance to prepare a manuscript. But oh, how I feel the lack of those long, youthful years when I should have been practicing the high art of public speaking!

For it is a high art. It gives unexcelled opportunities to impress oneself upon other lives, to be helpful and inspiring, to pass on to those that need it whatever blessing God has bestowed upon us. Freely we have received in order that we may give as freely, and we cannot give our thoughts freely if we are hampered by manuscripts.

Therefore, if I were young again I should follow Edward Everett Hale's shrewd advice, "Always make a speech whenever anyone is fool enough to ask you." Opportunities for practicing public speaking come often to young people to-day. There is the literary society of the public school. There is the Christian Endeavor society of the church. There are numerous other occasions greatly diversified in their nature, such as class meetings and "stunts" at social gatherings. All of these furnish priceless chances for practicing public speaking.

Do not allow yourself to be foolishly timid. Remember whom you are addressing—not one in the crowd that you would be afraid to speak to singly; why, then, fear them when bunched together?

Make preparation whenever you have advance notice, but let it be preparation of careful thought and orderly arrangement of the thoughts that come, rather than the committing to memory of certain sentences. Write, by all means, but only to clarify your mind, never to preserve and read what you have written. If you take to your speaking any writing, let it never extend beyond the barest outline of your speech, just a few key words. If possible, dispense with even these. Freedom and mastery of yourself and your audience come when you rely solely on the thought which you have made an inseparable part of yourself. Let words clothe the thought as they will.

Never seek after "fine" speaking. It is happily out of style and it never was effective. Seek for fine thought, and express it as simply and in as straightforward a manner as possible. Did you hear Lord Robert Cecil on his tour of the United States in the interest of the League of Nations which he did so much to establish? If you did, you will know how simply and clearly a forceful personality expresses itself.

And finally, place back of all your public speaking the strong reënforcement of religion. Remember Christ's promise to be with his disciples when they are called upon to testify for him in public, and claim that promise with an honest conscience. Never speak except for a good cause, and then you can depend upon Christ, the Master Orator, to give you words.

IV

If I Were Young Again

I Would Learn One Thing Well

IN saying that if I were young again I would learn one thing well, I do not, of course, mean to imply that I never learned one thing well; but I mean a big thing, something big enough to make a life foundation. In looking back over my sixty years, I see this as a decided lack, and I want to warn others against it.

The idea of specializing had not yet reached the college I attended. The curriculum was the same for all. I got a smattering of all sorts of sciences, of Greek and Latin and French and German and English, of the histories of all lands ancient and modern, of the various mathematics from arithmetic to calculus, of philosophy and political economy and ethics; in short, I was required to make a very sketchy little encyclopedia of myself. Then I went to teaching in the same college, and taught, first and last, about one dozen of the subjects I had "pursued."

The result is that I cannot read with pleasure in any language but my own, or speak an intelligible sentence in any other tongue. I am interested in all sciences, but am not at home in any. History fascinates me, but no historical period or national history is familiar to me. My mathematics is a thing of the forgotten past. My entire college course remains perhaps as "culture," but as culture so very general that it is about useless.

Now I would give all my sciences for one science so thoroughly mastered that I could go forth and do things in it; for botany, for instance, made so intimately my own that every tree and flower and fern and grass would be an individual, recognized friend. And I would give my two ancient and two modern languages (besides English) for a single language, say French, in which I could talk and write, read and think. And so with all the rest of my college course.

Life is too short for smatterings. As I review my sixty years I see that they would have been all too brief for botany—and think of trying to cram into them geology and astronomy, chemistry and physics, zoölogy and physiology and psychology and the other ologies! I might have become a respectable French scholar, or have gained a decent knowledge of American history, or have learned something worth while about political economy; I might have done any one of these things in sixty years, but hardly two of them, and as to all of them, each defeated the other.

My training fitted me for perhaps the one sole thing I finally undertook—journalism; for an editor has to write a little, but only a little, on all kinds of subjects, and seem wise, without necessarily being wise, in a multitude of matters. But even as it is, I am constantly brought into contact with specialists, with men and women who are thorough in one thing; and I have envied them their sense of mastery, their calm satisfaction in one little kingdom which each has made his own.

That is what counts—not so much knowing many flowers and trees and ferns and grasses as subduing one province of human knowledge. Take snail shells. When I was young I made a collection of these fascinating objects, all I could find in my Ohio neighborhood. But I did not go on from there and become a snail specialist. Why, by this time, I might know more about snails than anyone else in the world! The snails would not help me edit, but the sense of mastery would, the knowledge that in at least one little department I had something to give, and need not hold out my hat to anyone.

This joy of conquest permeates the entire life. No matter how tiny the subject which you have mastered; it may be only pins—and I have no doubt that I have hit upon a very big and complicated matter for an example —but the feeling that you have made the subject wholly your own will dignify and ennoble and strengthen your entire being and all your acts. That is why it is grandly worth while to specialize.

Let me make it very plain that I am not decrying general information, or the gaining of a smattering of many things. That is all we can do with most subjects in this busy world. But the thorough knowledge of some one thing will put all these smatterings in their true place, will teach you what real scholarship is, and will give you a happy sample of genuine achievement. We cannot do all things with equal thoroughness—life is too short for that—but we can know by experience of one thing what it is to be splendidly thorough, and the experience will be worth all it costs.

V

If I Were Young Again

I Would Train My Hands

NOW that I am sixty years old, I realize more than ever before what a mistake I made in my youth in not training my hands.

Of course I do not mean that when a boy I folded my hands and did nothing. I ran a lawn mower and used a sickle and a rake and a hoe. I sawed wood by the cord, and split it. I drove an occasional nail and put in an occasional screw. I made the emergency repairs that fall to the lot of the only masculine member of a family not at all well supplied with money. But my hands were not trained.

That is, though I could run a lawn mower, I could not adjust it, repair it, or sharpen it. Though I could saw oak and hickory logs, I could not set and sharpen my saw. If our steps gave way, we had to get a carpenter to build some new steps. If a ceiling was discolored, we had to send for the plasterer to whitewash it. If a hole was worn in a tin pail, it had to go to the tinner. If a shrub was to be set out, the nurseryman must do it. If a clock stopped, I must take it to the jeweler's.

I learned to set type, but set it slowly. I learned to typewrite, but with only a few of my fingers, and without being able to repair and adjust the machine. I pumped the college organ, but had to stop pumping if anything went wrong with the bellows. I rang the college bell, but when the boys stole the clapper, as they did about once a year, I was not the one to put in a new clapper. I was not at all lazy, nor was I too proud to work, but I was too clumsy and practically too ignorant to work to the best advantage.

When I became a college professor, some of my associates in the faculty won my envy and admiration by their facility in using tools. They could make chests of drawers, all of which would lock with a single key. They fashioned hymn-book racks for the chapel, and rebuilt the campus fence, for ours was a poor college. But I, with the best intentions in the world, could do none of these things. If I did anything, it was only the unskilled part that any clodhopper could do.

This college experience of mine has been continued through my life. At this very minute I am sitting in the back seat of my automobile writing this article while a mechanic, hastily summoned by telephone, is at work over the engine, trying to discover why it has stalled and left me stuck by the roadside. My neighbor would long ago have located the broken wire, and have gone smartly on his way. I am obliged to sit here, look as if I understood the mechanic's remarks about "condenser" and "distributor" and "timer" and "switch," and move off — no one knows when.

That is one reason why, if I were young again, I would train my hands, because if my hands were trained I should be more independent in a thousand ways than I am to-day. I should not be obliged to wait for other workmen. I could attend to matters in my own way as well as at my own time. I should save a lot of money and time and temper. I should be my own master.

But more than that, I should develop myself if I trained my hands. A young child develops mentally in large part through the action of his hands serving as stimulus to his brain. So it is that mechanical activity all through life stimulates thought and quickens the spirit. "All work and no play makes Jack a dull boy," but all play and no work makes Jack a duller boy. Manual training is not far from mental training, and it has important relations to religious training as well. An all-round life is the only sound life.

But I would remember another proverb, "Jack of

all trades, and master of none." I would select the kind of manual work that pleased me best, and try to become reasonably expert in that, calling in artisans for other labors. Cabinetwork, plumbing, gardening, electricity —whatever it might be—I would try to master it sufficiently for ordinary purposes. Then I should be able to look other artisans in the face and meet them on their own ground.

Perhaps it is not too late, even at sixty, but I am afraid it is. Arts learned readily at sixteen come hard at sixty. Time that is oceanic at sixteen has dwindled to a thin stream at sixty. The best I can do, I fear, is to pass this good advice along to my successors: Train your hands while you are young!

VI

IF I WERE YOUNG AGAIN

I WOULD BECOME EXPERT IN SOME SPORT

AS one grows older, it is said, the habit of talking about oneself is liable to grow. Having reached the age of sixty, I have probably formed that habit, and I fear I am illustrating it in these chapters. But I will try to talk about myself no more than is necessary to make my points, especially since what I am obliged to say about myself is what no one would be proud to report.

For example, as I look back over my sixty years, I am not at all proud of the way I have been playing. I inherited from my father, who was a great outdoor man, a fondness for outdoor life and athletic games, but I have been—and am—a "duffer" in every one of those outdoor sports that I have tried.

I like to attribute this to my nearsightedness; but then, my father also was nearsighted, but was a good horseback rider, a good hunter, a good swimmer, and a fair expert in other outdoor sports. I tried football, and when the big leather spheroid smashed in my face and shattered my glasses, I rightly concluded that it was too dangerous. I tried baseball and had precisely the same experience—with another pair of glasses; so I gave up baseball. I tried tennis, and, after years of effort, decided that that ball, though not at all a peril, was far too swift for my blundering vision, which was doubtless very true.

But there are other athletic sports better adapted to a nearsighted man. There is bowling, which I took up steadily for two winters; but I did not take the instruction I sadly needed, and even now I am quite as likely to miss all the pins as to knock down even one or two of them. There is bicycle-riding, which I followed for fully twenty years, but solely to "get there," and with, at the end, when the cycle "went out," no more thorough mastery of the fine points of the wheel than when I started. To-day there is the automobile, which I have been running for a decade, and still I do not know enough about the automobile engine to bring out in driving the best the makers put into it.

I am a devotee of walking, and can do my ten miles without turning a hair; but I have never developed myself with really long and systematic walks. There is horseback riding; but I have quit that, since a saddle turned under me and I broke a wrist. There is swimming, and my summer home is by the sea, but still any ten-year-old can get through the water faster than I can. There is running, for which my long legs would seem to equip me; but I am winded in half a minute, and stay winded. Just now there is golf, which would seem to be perfectly adapted to old boys of sixty; but I have been at it four or five years and my game is still atrocious, so that in despair I am taking lessons and am learning how stiff one can grow in six decades.

And so it is with indoor sports, to say merely a word about them. I have tried them all, but have not stuck with any of them long enough, or patiently enough, or with guidance enough to win the skill which is necessary for real and permanent enjoyment. Checkers would seem to be a simple game, but any checker expert can lay me out and not half try. Chess is a royal game and I am very fond of it, but a real chess player sees through my childish moves in a second, and mates me as fast as his fingers can move his men. Crokinole, halma, ping-pong, and all the rest—the story is the same. I believe in sports, and I do not know enough about any one sport to get much out of it or to enjoy it in the best way.

This personal confession carries its own moral. If I had my life to live over again, I would try for expertness in one indoor recreation and one outdoor sport. I think I would choose chess for indoors and running for outdoors,

If I Were Young Again

but my choice would depend upon circumstances. I would not confine myself to these two, of course, but I would specialize in them. I would get all I could from books, from observation, from personal instruction, and I would practice, practice, practice. I would not care for competition, for prizes, for "beating," but I would aim at technical mastery. Victories would come in their own time, but this mastery of the sport would be the only victory I would seek. And all this would be, not making drudgery of sport, but making it the kind of recreation that really re-creates.

22

VII

If I Were Young Again

I Would Read More Methodically

BOOKS have always been my delight. From my boy-hood days in Ohio—alas, how many years back!—when I sprawled out on the floor or the grass over Dickens or Scott or Thackeray, down to the present time of books of all sorts heaped up for review, reading has been my chief pleasure, and my library my unfailing resource. The collecting of books has also been a hobby. It started some fifty years back, when John B. Alden, of precious memory (and the good man is still alive) rejoiced the hearts of all thin-pursed youths by his reprints of great books at little prices, down to this present year when I gloat over a library of twenty thousand book friends.

And, in the main, my chief inspiration for life's tasks has come from books, and I owe them an immeasurable debt. Whatever blame I may cast on my reading, I have no fault to find with my books. Their wisdom was ready for wise reading, but my reading was not of the wisest.

My reading was ardent enough, persistent enough, thorough enough. I read by the hour, yes, by an aggregate of months in every year. I skipped no word. I copied much into my books of extracts. I read my favorites over and over. I gained a real knowledge of the books that struck my fancy. But I did not read methodically, and so I gained from my reading only a small part of what I might have gained.

As chance threw a good book in my way, I devoured it. Thus I read many good books, but on an amazing variety of subjects. And no subject was followed out so that I really knew something about it.

Take history, for example. I recall my joy in Motley's "Rise of the Dutch Republic," that vivid picture of

William of Orange, his noble character and his splendid struggles. But I did not read more about the history of the Netherlands, so that my mental picture of the Prince of Orange has no background or foreground. In the same way I exulted in Irving's "Conquest of Granada," but came away with nothing but a confused memory of knights and battles and no more real conception of the story of Spain than I had when I started. Thus also I read Irving's inspiring life of Washington and Holland's still more inspiring biography of Lincoln, but did not follow them up with the reading of enough books about the Revolution and the Civil War to make me at home in either epoch.

In short, though I have read scores, yes, hundreds of histories and biographies, I have no real satisfaction in thinking of any great historical character and his times such as I would have had if I had read, say, concerning one fifth as many persons or nations, and read five times as much about any one of them.

In the same way all my reading, which has been very extensive, has been desultory, and so has lost much of its value. I have read much fiction, but now an English story, now an American tale, now a Victorian novel, now one of this year's mintage, now a translation from some other language; and the result has been no understanding of the imaginative writings of any one country or period. I have read much poetry, but can quote very little, and that not accurately, nor am I thoroughly familiar with the works of any great poet, such as Shakespeare, Milton, or Dante. Many volumes of popular science have passed under my eyes, and I have skimmed them all with delight; but if I had devoted myself to a single science and read thoroughly in it, I might have a fair knowledge of it.

It is a common impression that simply reading is enough, no matter what you read. It is a still more common impression that if you read good books, you are sure to become wise. Nothing is farther from the truth. The missing element in the reading program of most of us is a sensible plan, persistently followed out. That, if the books are wisely chosen, will produce fine results in character and scholarship and solid, enduring pleasure; but haphazard reading of even the best books never will.

Therefore, if I were young again I would make a choice among the thousands of lines of reading open to me, and I would pursue some one of them long enough and far enough to get somewhere. If it were the history of the United States—and it might well be—I would read several of the best histories in order to familiarize myself with the general outline, and then fill it in by copious reading of books on special epochs and leading characters until I began to feel at home in the history of my own country, and could think and talk intelligently about it. Then I should have a nucleus about which all my later reading would cluster and to which it would cling. It is too late—perhaps—for me to do this; but it is not too late for you.

VIII

If I Were Young Again

I Would Select My Calling Earlier

IN these chapters I have had to make my points by writing about myself, which I do not like to do, though it may be considered the privilege of one who has reached the mature age of sixty. I am afraid that in this chapter I shall be obliged to write more about myself than in any of the former chapters, which is a pity; but it is all finding fault with myself, and holding myself up as a horrible example, so it is not quite so bad.

While I was in college I had not the slightest idea what I was going to make of myself. I took the studies as they came along, and did not choose my course with any thought of my future work. The college suspended operations for a year, and I found a country school to teach. College reopened and I went back and graduated. Still I had nothing in mind. I was asked to stay on in the college as a member of the faculty, and I did, for nine years, teaching all over the curriculum, and knowing one subject about as well as another. All I can say is, I managed to keep a little ahead of my classes. Then out of the blue sky came an invitation to become editor of the national Christian Endeavor paper, and I have been doing that for more than three decades. Few editors in the United States have been on their jobs longer than I. But—and this is the point—every single day of those three decades I might have done my work better if I had prepared for it during my school years and the years I spent as a college professor.

I know, of course, that it is neither possible nor wise to bend all our education to a single end. Much of it is for general culture; much of it is to give us broad views and ready sympathies and quick appreciation of all that is beautiful and noble. I would be the last to deprecate this general training, and to suggest the pouring of life into a single mold.

Also I know that sometimes one's likings and aptitudes change from decade to decade, so that what youth regards as the most desirable calling is seen by the mature man to be not at all the best thing for him to do. We cannot force our natures into tasks that are wholly uncongenial, even though we have trained ourselves for them, and it is better to shift from one calling to another than to remain in employments for which we have proved to be unfit.

Remembering all this, nevertheless I would insist that I made a mistake in not earlier fixing on some definite career, and focusing upon it. Numberless helps would have come to me if I had been on the watch for them, numberless suggestions, a host of stimulating thoughts and plans.

It is a common experience with me to decide on the subject for an article, and as soon as I have done this, though the subject may be quite out of my ordinary channels, to find ideas, facts, illustrations, quotations, all kinds of material for that article come flooding in upon me. Almost every book I open, every periodical I see, appears to have been written with that article in view. My friends edge around to it in their conversations, though not one of them knows that I am to write about it. The choice of a subject to write on seems to be a great magnet, drawing toward my life and mind just what I need to fill the essay.

Exactly this experience would have been mine if I had early decided upon my life work. Suppose I had decided to be an editor. I should have made the acquaintance of editors; I should have made a study of all the papers and periodicals I could obtain; I might have taken a correspondence course in journalism, if they had known such things in those days. Certainly I should not have spent ten or twelve years on Greek; I should have spent more time on history, political economy, and English literature.

Therefore I always advise young people to decide as early as possible, at least tentatively, what they are going to do in life. Even if their choice changes, the focused preparation which they will have made will not be lost. It will have given them the habit of looking ahead, of making mental accumulations related to definite subjects, of directing their life powers toward a certain end. And if the life choice is adhered to, they will have put back of it the golden formative years, the years of friendship-making, the years of habit-fixing, the years of first impressions. All of this will be of priceless value in a successful life.

IX

If I Were Young Again

I Would Join the Church Earlier

AGAIN, in order to make my point, I must give a little of my personal history. I was brought up in close association with the Presbyterian Church. I found in the church service, especially the sermon, a great delight. I rejoiced in the Sunday school, and attended it regularly. I also greatly enjoyed the prayer meeting, though it was a meager service, and did not often miss it.

Growing up, I became the Sunday-school librarian, and held other minor offices; I think I was superintendent of the school for a brief time, but I am not sure. For many years I taught a Sunday-school class. I sang in the church choir, and after a while became its leader. I began to take part in the church prayer meeting and usually was the only person besides the preacher who opened his mouth in that forlorn gathering. And yet I did not join the Church. My dear sister joined early, but I did not follow her good example. Finally I became a college professor, and had to take my turn in conducting chapel exercises and sometimes in preaching a sermon on Sunday; yet I was not a Church member.

The matter was not urged on me. Once my pastor asked me to join, in a hesitating way, and was apparently content when I said that I meant to sometime. Every year, when I was a boy, my Sunday-school teacher, a sainted woman, wrote me a letter urging me to join the Church; but I never answered those letters, by voice or pen. Once, later, one of my college professors asked me, after class, whether I called myself a Christian or not; and when I said I did, he also was content. That was all the urging I had to join the Church.

But the Christian Endeavor Society came along, and I joined with eagerness. I went into the Christian

Endeavor work most heartily, and after a while I began speaking before Christian Endeavor conventions. There I found, as I listened, that others were not satisfied, as I was, to assert that one could be a Christian outside the Church. At one meeting of the Ohio Christian Endeavor Union, a meeting of officers—I have forgotten how I happened to be there, for I hardly think I was an officer—everyone in the little room was asked to name his Church, and I had to say that I did not belong to any Church. I saw the inconsistency of my position and went home with my mind made up to join the Church before I went to another Christian Endeavor convention. I went at once to my pastor, came before the session, and joined the Church at the next communion service. I suppose there are millions who, like myself, have been led into Church membership by the Christian Endeavor Society.

But there I was, a college professor, having back of me a good many years of Sunday-school teaching, prayer-meeting speaking, and association with young folks. All that time I might have been influencing others to take a full and open stand for their Saviour, and I could not do it because I was not doing it. All the time, though in a way I was letting my light shine, it had this bushel basket turned over it. All that time, whatever of good example I might set, worked, in part, the wrong way; for the young folks said, "There is Professor Wells; he can be good without joining the Church, and so can I." The more folks liked me, the less they felt that Church membership was a wise and necessary thing.

I used to pretend that certain mysterious questions and doubts kept me out of the Church; but that was a mere blind, for I had found in the college library a copy of Mark Hopkins's "Evidences of Christianity," and that was too much for my skepticism. The truth of the matter was that I was very timid, and I kept hesitating over getting up before the church and becoming the center of public interest in that solemn ceremony of joining the Church. When I came to do it, I experienced not the slightest embarrassment, and all my worry about it was foolish and unwarranted; but it existed, and workers with young people seldom realize, because the young folks will never confess it, that they do not join the Church simply because they are "scared to."

So you see why, on looking back over my sixty years of life, one of the things I would certainly change is this: I would join the Church early. The chief reason is that I see clearly that my Lord and Redeemer wants his followers to join his Church. The second reason is that I see why he wants it. I see that Church membership makes the Christian life vastly easier and pleasanter and more effective. I see that every follower of Christ needs the Church as much as the Church needs him. And I see that every month's delay is a month that robs Christ of his due of outspoken loyalty and robs the Christian of his possibilities of satisfactory life.

X

If I Were Young Again

I Would Live for Larger Interests

A^S I look back on my life from the viewpoint of sixty years, it seems to me to lack one thing that I might very easily have put into it, and I will speak about it for the sake of the young folks who will read this chapter; because no one of them need make my mistake. I mean that I have been devoting my life needlessly to a very large number of small and even petty matters, and have not unified it with a big interest.

This error began in my boyhood and youth. I was devoted to a lot of little things. My collection of butterflies and moths absorbed much of my time. But so also did my collection of beetles, and my collection of stamps, and my collection of postmarks, and my collection of snail shells, and my collection of the teeth of various animals, and my collection of pressed flowers, and my collection of tree buds and twigs, and my collection of leaves, and various other collections, the chief of which was my collection of minerals and fossils. I might have chosen one of these and made it a big interest, but there were too many of them for anything but pottering. It would also be very difficult for an ordinary fellow, not a scientific genius, to develop any of these into a big interest. I certainly did not. These collections, the gathering and handling of so many hundreds of little things, taught me to think in small ways rather than in large. That is the danger of collecting that is merely collecting, no matter what one collects.

Then I made a tremendous number of newspaper clippings, which I pasted into voluminous scrapbooks and classified in numerous envelopes. This is a useful habit if it is not carried too far, and if the clippings are not too wide in their scope. But I clipped whatever interested me, and I seem to have been interested in about everything printed. Naturally my house became —and is still—overburdened with great masses of bits of folded paper which I have no time or strength to arrange, and not very much need to consult if they ever should be arranged. They are potentially very valuable —to some one; and so I do not throw them away. They occupy scores of great boxes in the attic.

This is only a part of the story. I have already written in this series of chapters about the many sports I tackled, the many books I read, the many studies I undertook, carrying none of them very far, and becoming one of the most discursive smatterers, I suppose, who ever lived.

And all this while the biggest kind of big things were offering themselves to me.

It is amazing how unconscious I was of them all. I grew up without knowing the location or characteristics of a single railroad system. Their initials, rattled off so glibly by my accomplished intimates, were worse than Greek to me, for I did know Greek; but I did not know the B. & O. from the N. Y., N. H. & H., or the Union Pacific from the Southern Pacific. I did not know the character of a single big newspaper. Of congressmen, members of the Cabinet, Supreme Court judges, and the like I was serenely ignorant. I never read the platform of a political party, and was a red-hot Republican by prejudice only, and not in the least by information (in which, to be sure, I was far from alone).

Meanwhile, other young fellows all around me were developing large interests. Some of them went head and heels into the temperance reform, and have since helped to carry it to a measure of success which has amazed the world and astonished themselves. I kept outside of that great interest. Some of them have devoted themselves to politics, and are now doing big things for the state and the nation. Some have gone into social reform, and have remedied awful miseries, corrected hideous wrongs, founded large benefices, added greatly to the sum of human happiness, safety, and comfort. I kept away from social-settlement work, from home missions and foreign missions, from evangelism, from applied political economy and sociology. I admired Jacob A. Riis and Frances E. Willard and John B. Gough and Henry Bergh and Clara Barton and the other great leaders of my day —admired them from a distance, that is—but I did not enlist under their banners.

To be sure, I have been called into two very big things, the national Christian Endeavor work and Sunday-school work, and I am grateful to those that have, as it were, forced me into contact with these large and fundamental interests; but even here I can hardly say that I have dealt with affairs in a broad and constructive way, but rather as a recorder of the work of others; the old habit of collecting, you see.

And so I feel like saying to all young people: Associate yourself with some big human interest, some large effort to help mankind and improve human conditions; not necessarily as a leader—few have the opportunity or the ability for leadership—but anyone can become a glorious follower. As big things are now waiting to be done as ever have been done in the world. The one matter of the abolition of war, for example, and the establishment of a safe, just, progressive, and thoroughly Christian civilization on earth, is the biggest thing mankind ever has undertaken, and it must be done soon, or mankind will perish. Get into some big thing. You will do the little things all the better for it.

XI

If I Were Young Again

I Would Work More for Others

I IMAGINE that most men, when they reach my age of sixty and look back over their lives, wish that they had done more for others. By this time, many who were nearest and dearest to me have gone to their eternal home, and I would give much if I could remember more kindnesses that I had done for them. The kindnesses I did do, that I can recall, stand out as the most blessed satisfactions in my memory; and they might easily have been more numerous. As I look back over the decades, I can see countless opportunities for helpfulness that I missed. There were many burdens, as I know now, that I was too selfishly blind to see; many sorrows that I was too much absorbed in my own work to perceive and to sympathize with. If I could be young again, knowing what I know now, I am sure I should do more for my dear ones.

There is something else that men realize as they "get along in years," and that is that among all their friends and acquaintances, however many and valued, it is in the main the old friends that count for the most. We understand this as they begin to drop away from us, and sometimes we understand it long before that. Usually we comprehend the preciousness of friendship after it is too late to make many of the best kinds of friendships, those that will carry into the sunset years the memories and the glow of youth. Millions of men come to old age and suddenly find that they are quite alone in the world. They may have had a crony or two, but they are gone. Only the younger folks are left, very dear and precious, of course, but of another generation, with quite new and often quite strange ideas and tastes, and with none of the sweet memories that one likes to recall. The worst of it is that if we had made more friends in our youth, a host of them would go down to old age with us, and we should not be lonely at all.

And in the third place, there are the thousands of little by-the-way kindnesses, done not to those nearest to us, not to relatives and friends, or even to acquaintances, but to casual passers-by, to those we meet in railway stations, to fellow pedestrians on crowded streets, to beggars, to sick folk, to little children, to people who are plainly lonely and discouraged and forlorn. As I look back over my sixty years, I know that I have let myriads of such opportunities get by me.

Every one of them was an opportunity to please my Saviour. He has identified himself with earth's forlornities, with all earth's needy ones. When I am the only one in my automobile, and I see an old man trudging painfully in the direction I am going, and do not give him the cheery lift that means so little to me and so much to him, I am missing a chance to have Jesus Christ with me in my car. When I see a worried mother leaving a train with three or four little children and a heavy valise, if I hurry past her to my office, I am missing a chance to carry one of my Lord's burdens for him. When I see a little chap crying by the roadside, and dash by him without a word of comfort or perhaps of timely admonition, I am missing a chance to receive one of Christ's little ones, and thus of receiving Christ himself into my life.

As I review these sixty years, I am really afraid to estimate how many of these blessed opportunities I have heedlessly scorned. These lost chances explain in part a certain coldness and lack of joy in my religious life. I might have come so much closer to the Source of all warmth and happiness in the persons with whom he would have entered. Alas, for my thousands of neglected opportunities!

If I Were Young Again

It is never too late to begin living unselfishly, and I am trying to change the habits that I realize I have been forming through six decades; but sixty years stiffen character, and render exceedingly difficult what would otherwise by this time have become a charming and simple instinct. I am writing to those that need not, must not, make my mistake. Begin now. Look more eagerly for chances to do kindnessess than you look for favors for yourself. Get into the way of giving—gifts of loving sympathy and of lavish time as well as of what money and other possessions you have. Practice it. Persist in it. Though it is hard, work at it until it grows easy. Take my word for it, based on thorough knowledge but on sadly little experience, that such giving of yourself will prove the most glorious income you could possibly crowd into your treasury.

XII

If I Were Young Again

I Would Give More Time to Soul Nurture

ONE of the things that I chiefly regret as I review the sixty years of my life is that I have spent so little time in feeding my soul. I have written many books on soul nurture, and I have given much good advice to others; but for the most part I have been too busy writing the advice to take it myself. As I look back over my years, I seem always to have my pen in my hand, exhorting others through the printed page. I cannot parallel my working existence with any such stretch of prayer, of Bible-reading, of meditation on great truths, of vital communion with my Redeemer.

Men who have given the most help to the world have been those that have not stinted the food they have fed to their spirits. They have been men of the Book. They have read the Bible, not by single verses or paragraphs hurriedly snatched at irregular intervals, but by books at a time, hearty meals of Scripture, built into the blood and bone and muscle of their souls. No wonder they have had spiritual stamina. No wonder they have been sturdy for hard work and as firm as a rock in times of temptation and of stress.

Such men, too, have been men of prayer. They have not mumbled the Lord's Prayer at night, and made two or three meager petitions in the morning. They have sat down for long and full talks with their Elder Brother, they have gone over with him all their trials and perplexities, they have referred to him all their doubts and fears, they have thanked him for all their joys and opportunities, they have lived their lives over with him. So blessed have been these daily experiences that they have looked forward to them with great longing and remembered them with profound satisfaction. As two human friends want to be together all they can be, and talk with each other as long as possible, so they with their Lord.

And the men that have been the greatest blessing to the world have thought much about their God and his mercies, their duty, the eternal life before them, their sins, their salvation, and their Saviour. They have not lived haphazard lives. They have planned far in advance, they have planned for the endless years. They have built love and courage and faith and hope into their subconscious minds. The fundamental principles of Christian character have not been to them mere names in a book, but parts of their inmost selves. In our bustling age we are likely to forget and lose altogether the art of meditation; these most helpful men find much time for it.

Nor do such men expect to get along without other men in their soul nurture. They rejoice in sermons, in prayer meetings, in Christian conversations, in uplifting books. They surround themselves with ennobling influences. They gather into their minds and hearts all they can reach of fine thoughts and inspiring examples. They turn the whole world into a school for the nurture of their spirits, and they have for their teachers a myriad of glorious books and glorious Christians.

Because I have neglected so much of this, I am anxious that others shall not neglect it while they are young. I am taking time for it now; how ardently I wish that years ago I had taken time for it!

The busiest life can find a chance to eat three meals a day, and will not think of starving the body. Not the busiest life that ever was lived need starve the soul. Time spent in eating is not wasted; without it we should soon be at the end of our time on earth. Neither is time wasted that is spent in eating soul food; without it we shall be losing not earth time, but a vast eternity.

Even earth time, however, is saved by soul nurture.

Half an hour of prayer is quite sure to bring rich returns in the secular as well as in the spiritual life; our time is better directed, our efforts are more persistent and far more fruitful. The best economy of time and strength is to employ them liberally in the education and training of the spirit.

Here I come to the end of this series of chapters. I have talked much about myself, but surely not egotistically. I have confessed many failures and errors, in order that you young folks may avoid them. Do not wait sixty years for it, or forty years, or one year. Begin now to build up a strong body, to store your memory with noble expressions of noble thoughts, to practice public speaking, to learn at least one thing well, to train your hands, to become expert in some sport, to read methodically, to choose your life work, to live for larger interests, to work more for others; above all, join the Church now, if you have not already taken your stand openly for Christ, and give more time to the nurture of your soul. These are the twelve things I wish I had done when I was young; make them twelve things that you will not leave undone.

www.ingramcontent.com/pod-product-compliance
Lightning Source LLC
Chambersburg PA
CBHW030308030426
42337CB00012B/636